P9-DJK-566

SIMON & SCHUSTER BOOKS FOR YOUNG READERS • An imprint of
Simon & Schuster Children's Publishing Division • 1230 Avenue of the Americas,
New York, New York 10020 • Copyright © 2013 by Meghan McCarthy • All rights
reserved, including the right of reproduction in whole or in part in any form. • SIMON
& SCHUSTER BOOKS FOR YOUNG READERS is a trademark of Simon & Schuster, Inc. • For
information about special discounts for bulk purchases, please contact Simon &
Schuster Special Sales at 1-866-506-1949 or business@simonandschuster.com.
The Simon & Schuster Speakers Bureau can bring authors to your live event.
For more information or to book an event, contact the Simon & Schuster Speakers Bureau
at 1-866-248-3049 or visit our website at www.simonspeakers.com. • Book design by
Chloë Foglia • The text for this book is set in Korinna. • The illustrations for this book are
rendered in acrylic paint. • Manufactured in China
0313 SCP
10 9 8 7 6 5 4 3 2 1
Library of Congress Cataloging-in-Publication Data
McCarthy, Meghan. • Daredevil / Meghan McCarthy.—1st edition. • p. cm
"A Paula Wiseman Book."
Audience: Ages 4-8. • Audience: Grades K-3.
ISBN 978-1-4424-2262-9 (hardcover) • ISBN 978-1-4424-8188-6 (eBook)
1. Skelton, Betty—Juvenile literature. 2. Women air pilots—United States—
Biography—Juvenile literature. 3. Air pilots—United States—Biography—
Juvenile literature. 4. Automobile racing drivers—United States—Biography—
Juvenile literature. 5. Women automobile racing drivers—United States—
Biography—Juvenile literature. I. Title.
TL540.S5734M35 2013
629.13092—dc23
[B]
2012023603

DAREDEVIL

The Daring Life of Betty Skelton

Meghan McCarthy

54

A Paula Wiseman Book
Simon & Schuster Books for Young Readers
NEW YORK LONDON TORONTO SYDNEY NEW DELHI

W hile most girls played with their dolls, Betty Skelton played with her metal plane.

It was the early 1930s and airplanes were still very new . . . and exciting. Naval airplanes buzzed over the top of Betty's house, flipping and turning. Betty sat on her back steps and imagined that she was in the pilot's seat.

Betty and her family lived in Pensacola, Florida, which was near the sea. Luckily for Betty it was also near a giant navy base. On Sundays Betty's mom and dad drove her to view the navy airplanes up close.

That's when the family met Ensign Kenneth Wright. He introduced them to the joy of flight.

Betty yearned to know more. She wanted to touch the sky. When she was eight she mailed a letter to all the major airplane manufacturers. She later said that it read, "My father wants to buy an airplane. Please send me all the information." The pamphlets poured in. Betty studied them hard.

At the age of twelve her father boosted her up, plopped her into a plane, and waved good-bye. Betty was flying by herself!

"It wasn't quite legal then so I couldn't tell anybody," Betty later recalled. "But . . . it was amazing."

As Betty grew bigger, so did her dreams.
When most kids turn sixteen, they get a license to drive a car.

Betty got one to fly a plane!

She even made the newspaper.

Solo on Her 16th Birthday

RB

A red and white Taylor craft droned through the clouds, its shining wings reflecting the bright rays of the sun.

* * *

It was Sunday morning, June 28, and at the controls was Miss Betty June Skelton, who was celebrating her 16th birthday with her first solo flight.

* * *

"No, I wasn't nervous," she said, "I had been waiting too long to become of age, to feel afraid." Thus the auburn-haired girl with laughing brown eyes and a few scattered freckles on a pert nose spoke of her first solo.

Sixteen is the minimum age at which fliers may solo.

* * *

Miss Betty June Skelton, daughter of Mr. and Mrs. David Skelton, and the youngest member of the Eighth group of the Civil Air patrol with

Betty didn't just want to fly for fun.
She wanted to make it her career.

Although Betty wanted to be a commercial pilot, she couldn't. Only men could be commercial pilots in the late 1940s.

"I wanted very much to fly in the navy," Betty remembered, "but all they would do is laugh when I asked."

What was Betty to do?

Betty soon learned how to become a stunt pilot. She preferred to call what she did aerobatic flying because there was an art to it.

She soon became famous for the inverted ribbon cut. Betty would *swoop* toward the ground while upside down and cut a ribbon with her propeller. Amazing!

Betty never flew alone. Her dog, Little Tinker,
was always by her side.

Betty also flew barefoot. She liked for her feet to feel free.

At the age of twenty-two Betty fell in love with a very special plane—the smallest in existence. At first the owner didn't want to sell it to her because, as Betty put it, "she was a woman," but Betty's charm won him over.

"It's just the ship for a half-pint like me," Betty said. "I don't weigh one hundred pounds even when I'm soaking wet," she added. "I didn't just sit in that little airplane, I wore it. If I sneezed, it sneezed with me." She named the plane "Little Stinker."

In 1951 Betty set out to break an altitude record. It took some convincing to borrow the right plane for the job because, again, she was a woman. But the plane's owner relented, and Betty set off. Betty and the plane reached a record height of 29,050 feet, which is higher than the top of Mount Everest. The temperature outside was fifty-three below zero! "My feet darn near froze to death," Betty said.

Betty retired from flying in the early 1950s. "It was getting to be old stuff," Betty said. But she didn't relax for long.

Betty got into her first racecar in 1954 and off
she drove into a new career!

During Betty's racing days she borrowed her friend's Cyclops jet-powered car and raced on Utah's Bonneville Salt Flats. The land was a crust of white salt that blew into Betty's face as she raced.

This didn't stop Betty. "The car got airborne with me toward the end of the run," Betty remembered fondly. She broke the women's record with a speed of 315.74 mph!

Betty had broken records in the air and on the ground. She then moved on to the water . . .

. . . and became the first female boat jumper. (The surprise is that she couldn't swim!)

Betty was always up for a good challenge. She'd conquered the sky, the land, and the water. What would be next?

Then she got a call. Because Betty had broken so many records and was good at so many things, she was invited to be the first woman to train with male astronauts and . . . they were going to space! The group was called Mercury 7.

MALYSHKA

LINDA

Previously only animals had gone into outer space. No man—or woman—had yet done so. This was Betty's chance! "Golly, that would be the most fantastic thing in the world." Of course she'd go!

Could Betty be the one? Could she fly with the Mercury 7?

Look magazine put Betty on the front cover.
America was waiting!

Betty did all sorts of training. . . .

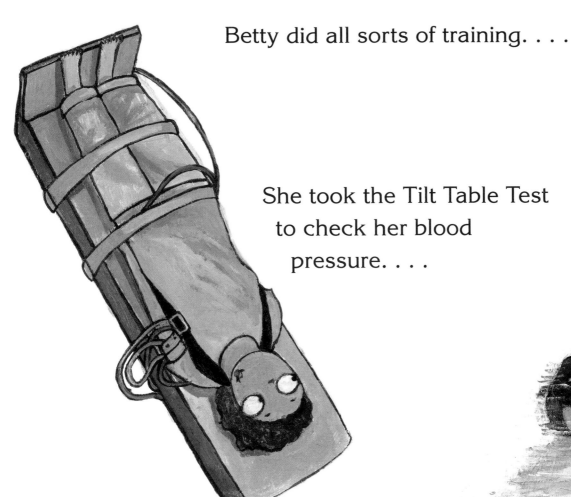

She took the Tilt Table Test
to check her blood
pressure. . . .

She spun in the Barany chair
until it would make most
people throw up. . . .

Even though Betty didn't know how to swim, she trained underwater to simulate weightlessness. "This was me during one of the water tests, which I was pleased didn't last very long," she said.

Betty was readying herself to rocket into space. . . .

The other astronauts welcomed her. They nicknamed her 7 and a half.

When it was time for the Mercury 7 to suit up, they put on their silver suits and their giant glass helmets . . .

Betty was left behind. She wasn't one of the Mercury 7. NASA wasn't ready to send a woman to space. Not just yet. But that didn't matter to Betty. She had proven that women could do it as well as men. Women CAN fly airplanes! They CAN drive cars really fast! They CAN go to space . . . and they did.

In 1963 Russian Valentina Tereshkova became the first woman and civilian in space.

In 1983 Sally Ride was the first American woman in space.

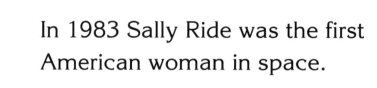

Thanks to Betty Skelton, their trips were possible.

Betty owned and drove a shiny red Corvette until the day she died. "I just like to go fast," Betty said. And she did.

© Beltman / CORBIS

During Betty's ribbon-cutting stunt, an audience member would be picked to hold one of the poles. Then Betty would swoop her plane toward the person with the pole, purposely scaring him or her! Of course he or she always dropped the pole. Then a trained professional would pick up the pole and Betty would fly at the ribbon again, this time cutting it. It was always a crowd pleaser and probably more than a tad bit scary for the person holding the pole!

Betty was a car design consultant for Dodge. She wanted cars to have a feminine touch.

Betty's secret ambition was to be a writer, said one newspaper from the 1940s.

In high school Betty was a cheerleader, a football sponsor, the class president, member of the national dramatic sorority, and had the leading role in the class play.

Betty's first Corvette was made of metallic gold, had a cream interior, and even had 14-karat-gold buckles with her name engraved, and a gold platform for her feet to rest on.

Betty rode motorcycles; jumped out of planes; flew jets, helicopters, gliders, and blimps, and drove hydroplanes.

You can see Betty's plane in person at the National Air and Space Museum in Washington, D.C.

Betty didn't tell her mom about her first solo flight for about a week!

Betty "fibbed" about her age and got a desk clerk job at Eastern Airlines three weeks before graduating from high school. She worked from midnight to eight so that she could fly during the daytime. "The only way I could fly was to work," Betty said.

Betty wore men's pajamas during space training because they didn't have anything in her size.

"I had quite a few close calls . . . but I can honestly say that I was never really afraid."

"My folks, I think, had always wanted a boy. My dad kind of led me more toward masculine things. He took me to boxing matches every Tuesday night and taught me how to box a little—so the girl down the street wouldn't pick on me. And my mother went right along with most everything I wanted to do."

Did Betty believe in aliens? In a 1999 interview she said, "In 1948 I became extremely interested in UFOs. A fellow named Keyhoe wrote a couple of books called *Flying Saucers Are Real* and *Flying Saucers from Outer Space* and I read every page and my father thought I was crazy."

"Any time now things are going to happen beyond our greatest imagination. I only wish I were twenty to thirty years younger to get in on more of it."

"Aerobats are murder on one's hairdo."

What did Betty like to eat? "I like Spanish foods, but sweets best of all. I usually nibble on candy all day long."

"I can't cook but I do design my own clothes."

Betty had this to say about her 1958 drive through the Andes in a Chevrolet station wagon: "It was extremely hazardous traveling. We went through a blizzard, a tornado, and over roads that could hardly be more than trails."

"I didn't date in high school because I was so busy with flying, and that was the most important thing to me."

Upon exiting a plane, Betty always had a pair of high heels waiting. She said, "I hate even to pose in my flying slacks, it looks so unladylike."

Betty test-drove cars for safety in the 1950s. She had this to say: "I'm completely wrapped up in the car industry. It's a field that touches the lives of so many people—and I like people."

What did Betty have to say about astronaut training? "It was the most exciting experience of my entire life! I made it through about twenty different tests. There were times when I thought that one roll or spin would be too much, and fortunately, the test would stop at that point."

"I just can't stand standing still."

Time Line

1926	Betty June Skelton is born!
1938	Betty flies solo
1942	She receives her private pilot's license at the age of sixteen
1944	Betty graduates from high school Becomes a certified flight instructor
1945	Joins the Civil Air Patrol (civilian support to help with the war effort)
1946	Begins her career as an aerobat and purchases her first plane, a Great Lakes 2T-1A biplane
1948	Becomes Feminine International Aerobatics Champion Betty buys the famous *Little Stinker*
1949	Sets unofficial world speed record for engine aircraft (426.5 mph) Wins Feminine International Aerobatics Champion
1950	Sets World Light Plane Altitude Record (25,763 feet) Wins Feminine International Aerobatics Champion
1951	Sets World Light Plane Altitude Record (29,050 feet) Retires from flying as a career
1954	First woman to drive an Indy Car Sets new world women's closed course record (144.02 mph) Sets Stock Car Flying Mile Record of 105.88 mph
1956	Becomes an advertising executive for Campbell-Ewald Sets new land speed record of 145.044 mph Sets transcontinental record from New York to Los Angeles: 56 hours, 58 minutes
1958	Sets South American Transcontinental Auto Speed Record: 41 hours, 14 minutes
1959	Trains with the Mercury 7 astronauts at NASA
1965	Marries her first husband, Donald Frankman, a commercial pilot and award-winning commercial TV director and producer. Sets new land speed record (315 mph)
1969	Becomes Vice President of Campbell-Ewald's new Women's Market and Advertising Department Successfully lobbies to end discrimination against female pilots in air racing
1977	Betty publishes her autobiography called *Little Stinker*
1985	Donates *Little Stinker* to the National Air and Space Museum
1988	Betty is the first woman to be inducted into International Aerobatic Hall of Fame
1993	The first woman to be inducted into NASCAR International Motorsports Hall of Fame Inducted into Florida Women's Hall of Fame
1997	Inducted into Women in Aviation Pioneer Hall of Fame
2001	The first woman to be inducted into Corvette Hall of Fame Inducted into National Aviation Hall of Fame Betty's husband Donald dies
2005	Betty marries her second husband, Dr. Allen Erde, a retired naval surgeon
2008	Inducted into the Motorsports Hall of Fame
2011	Betty dies August 31 at the age of eighty-five

© Meghan McCarthy

Selected Bibliography

For a complete bibliography and more visit: meghan-mccarthy.com.

"Aerobatic Champ Fly Midget Plane," *The Cincinnati Post*, 1949.

"Betty Skelton: Aerobatic pilot and race car driver who set so many altitude and speed records that she acquired the nickname the 'first lady of firsts'," *The Times* [London (UK)], September 24, 2011.

"Betty Skelton Calm On Space," *The Baltimore Sun*, June 18, 1963.

Betty Skelton Oral History Interview, C-Span Video Library, July 19, 1999, http://www.c-spanvideo.org/program/292945-1

Carlisle, Ronald, "How High Is Up?" *Sunday Mirror Magazine*, March 20, 1949.

"Girl, 19, Thrills Crowds As Aerobat," *Sunday Tribune*, August 4, 1956.

"Girl Sets U.S. Altitude Record for Small Planes," *The Washington Post*, January 9, 1949.

Hevesi, Dennis. "Betty Skelton, Air and Land Daredevil, Dies at 85," *New York Times*, September 10, 2011.

"Pretty Betty Skelton Succeeds—Superior in Masculine Fields," *Revere Lantern*, April 11, 1958.

Rawlings, Nate. "Betty Skelton," *Time* magazine, September 26, 2011.

Schudel, Matt. "Betty Skelton, 'Fastest Woman on Earth,' dies at 85," *The Washington Post*, September 3, 2011.

Shayler, David J., and Ian A Moule. *Women in Space – Following Valentina*, Springer Praxis Books/Space Exploration, 2005.

Smith, Corinne, "Unofficial Astronaut," *The Detroit News*, April 17, 1961.

Steindorf, Sara. "Daredevil Betty Skelton," *The Christian Science Monitor*, December 9, 1999.

Sutherly, Ben. "Aviation hall inductees 'changed the world'; Two men, two women earn place in national hall," *Dayton Daily News*, July 17, 2005.

"The Lady Wants to Orbit," *Look* magazine, February 2, 1960.